FAITH
AND FINANCE

UNDERSTANDING
THE INSEPARABLE LINK

JIM PALMER

Copyright 2007 Focus Press, Inc.

FAITH AND FINANCE
Published by Focus Press, Inc.

© Copyright 2007 Focus Press, Inc.
International Standard Book Number
978-0-9796356-2-5

Cover and interior design by Marc Whitaker
Cover image by Shutterstock

Scripture Quotations are from:

From The Holy Bible, English Standard Version
© copyright 2001 Crossway Bibles,
a division of Good News Publishers.
Used by permission. All rights reserved.

New King James Version (NKJV)
© copyright Thomas Nelson Publishers
Used with permission.

Printed in the United States of America
ALL RIGHTS RESERVED

For information, contact the publisher:
FOCUS PRESS, INC.
1600 WESTGATE CIRCLE
BRENTWOOD, TN 37027

Online at: focuspress.org

Contents

ACKNOWLEDGEMENTS

Without much encouragement, wise counsel, and incisive comments from the kindred spirits of close friends and family, this book would not be a reality. To say it was one of the most difficult projects I have ever completed would be an understatement. It has been an enriching, rewarding, and oftentimes arduous journey and I'm thankful for those who have helped me see it through.

Thanks to Brad Harrub, my trusted friend and constant "Barnabas" for helping me see the vision of putting these thoughts and principles into a book format in hopes that other lives might be blessed by them. Thanks to Tonja and Nathan McRady for spending the time to work through the grammatical minefields that were my first drafts. Thanks to my parents whose words of encouragement and training to persevere came in handy during this process. Thanks to my wife for her steadfast support and reassurance when it seemed like there would never be a light at the end of the tunnel. And, thanks be to God for blessing me with the ability and life experience to put these truths into practice and then onto paper.

PREFACE

Imagine for a moment that you have acquired a business. You are now the owner and operator of a bicycle manufacturing plant. Every day your company is in charge of producing bicycles – that's what you do. You own equipment and bicycle parts, and you have people who are commissioned with the task of assembling bike after bike after bike. You are excited about owning a business. You even like bikes! This is a surefire success, and you can't wait for your first day.

Month one passes and you encounter a problem at the plant: Every bike that is produced has three wheels. You realize you are producing tricycles, not bicycles. You scratch your head in wonder and exclaim, "I thought I had purchased a bicycle plant! Why are tricycles being produced?" Suddenly, you are faced with a decision: Will you do something about the problem?

But the first month has been so hectic and you have so much to do that you decide to put off doing anything about it. You think, "Next month will be less hectic, and if I still have this problem I'll look into it more fully." You decide, "Maybe it was a first month glitch. Maybe things will correct themselves." So you resolve to wait and watch; after all, things will surely work themselves out... no use worrying, right?

The next month passes. And it was busier than the first month. Your sales figures are abysmal; after all, people want bicycles, not tricycles. You simply hope things will get better next month.

Only the next month passes and you find out that the results are the same as prior months: Tricycles – not bicycles – are coming off the assembly line. Bills are due and sales are flat. What are you to do?

Unfortunately, many of us would do nothing. Oh, we might **hope** things get better. We might even **pray** for things to get better. However, far too few of us would take the time that we should, leave the office, go out into the plant and day by day walk through the operations. **Too few of us would take the time to find and correct the problem.**

Instead, we'd leave it to chance. We'd continue to do the same things we'd done the whole time – all the while hoping for different results. And while we might think things would change by themselves, this is wrong thinking. Without corrective measures, we would continue to get tricycles and our business would not only suffer, it would fail.

How do I know that many of us would continue down this path?

I know because many of us do it every day and every month with our diets, our exercises, our relationships, our jobs, our faith, and… our finances. We hope things will change, but many of us never actually take the steps that are necessary to instigate that change.

We are extremely busy. We think things will improve *next* month. That mountain of bills will surely get smaller *next* month. The meager savings account will surely grow *next* month. Your ability to give more to God and His good works through the Church will surely improve *next* month. And we hope and maybe even pray. Then we continue to do the same things we've done each month in the past and beat ourselves up for not getting a different result.

The problems arise due to a broken link, a link that God ordained as one that was to be inseparable. The link is between Faith and Finance and should never be abolished. Faith and Finance go together like hand in glove, peas and carrots, and Legos! You really can't discuss one without the other. They simply go together. Together is when they make the most sense. Together, Faith and Finance are a team that makes life work well, both here and in eternity.

Don't break the link: *Will you take the time to address and correct financial problems in your life?*

In the coming chapters, I hope to clearly identify the broken link that may be causing trouble in your life and then help you repair it. Or, if you already understand the link between Faith and Finance, maybe your faith will grow and your financial outlook will be "less burden and more blessing." I hope you will find the answers from God's Word to the questions that plague you when you think about Faith and Finance. By carefully examining the Scriptures, I pray that you will come to understand the inextricable link between the terms *Faith* and *Finance*. The purpose of this book is to examine and discuss the thoughts God would have us think regarding the important topic, money. All the while let us pay close attention to proper application in real life as a faithful Christian. Prayerfully, this book will provide you some direction by helping you look deeply into God's Word.

I believe that once we come to a proper understanding of how God would have us view and handle the blessing of money that we will shake off old ways of thinking and *doing*. I believe we will better understand the role money should play in our lives. I believe we will realize the inherent need to put – and keep – God first in our lives. And I believe the resulting life of peaceful prosperity will be beneficial to us, our families, and most of all – our God.

May God be glorified.

Jim

CHAPTER ONE

Is Money Your Servant
or Your Master?

> If we command our wealth, we shall
> be rich and free. If our wealth
> commands us, we are poor indeed.
> — British statesman, Edmund Burke

"I'll be wrapped around your finger...
I will turn your face to alabaster
Then you will find your servant is your master
And you'll be wrapped around my finger."

In 1983, written by Sting and sung by The Police, "Wrapped Around Your Finger" became a chart topping single. Characterized by mythological references and 17th century phrases, the theme of the song ultimately seems to be control. Initially, the *master* is in control of the apprentice – the apprentice is wrapped around the master's finger - but ultimately, the apprentice is able to wrest control and wrap the former master around *his* finger. At this point, the servant who was once employed to bring benefit to the master has now turned the tables and become, a ruthless master in the process.

So it goes with money.

In the beginning, money serves great and sundry purposes. Money is the medium of exchange that is required in order

might feed and be fed, clothe and be clothed, shel-
...d be sheltered. Money **is** important. Money **is** a bless-
...g. Ask the man, woman, or child who does not have
...money whether or not the last two statements are true.
Without money, one would starve, die of exposure, and be
homeless. Money's importance is above debate.

However, today maybe as in no society before, money (and the
quest for more of it) has replaced God, family, and health as priority number one. The quest to increase one's monetary possessions is sought with the passion once reserved for a pursuit of
God, faith, and the Truth. Many times one's family is left
unguided and undisciplined while dad, mom, or both, chase
down the dollar. Often, as a result of excessive amounts of time
being spent sitting at a desk, driving the highways and byways,
or pondering the latest "get rich quick" scheme, one's health
sags and ultimately gives way to preventable sickness and dis-
ease. Simply put: The power, prestige, and *feeling* of security
that comes from being wealthy are overwhelming influences on
people today. The love of money is ubiquitous. Americans are
inundated with it in the media. The pursuit of the dollar has
become a way of life for many. And Christians are not immune.

Link #1: *How much emphasis do you place on
money? Which would your children view as more
important to you: money or God?*

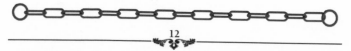

In Matthew 6:24, Jesus warned, "No one can serve masters; for either he will hate the one and love the oth or else he will be loyal to the one and despise the other. You cannot serve God and Mammon (riches)."

Who is your Master? Whom do you serve? Are you serving a ruthless taskmaster or the One whose yoke is easy and burden is light? For you, does money serve as a defense (Ecclesiastes 7:12), a means of protection and a blessing from the God of heaven (Ecclesiastes 5:18-19) or has the servant become your master?

Are you ready to take action, to take charge of your financial situation so that you can "do good, be rich in good works, be generous and share, thus storing up treasure for [yourself] as a good foundation for the future, **so that [you] may take hold of that which is truly life**" (1 Timothy 6:18-19, ESV, emp. added)?

Remember, the choice is ours. Each of us will give an account of how we have handled our lives, and our blessings, while here on this earth. Based on the master you are serving, what will be your eternal destiny? Now is the time for us to choose our master, to choose this day, whom we will serve (Joshua 24:15).

Link #2: Spend a few minutes looking over your checking account to "see" whom you have been serving in the past. If the evidence indicates that you have been mastered by your money take the steps needed to turn it around.

Thoughts for discussion

Servant or Master?

Money is a powerful force. It can be used for much good or it can be a force for evil. It can help its owner or it can harm. The pursuit of money and the power and influence money wields has caused countless problems in lives throughout history. And yet, it can be quite a blessing from God. It has the ability to gain control over one's life if it is allowed to take over. Write down some of the ways money might gain control over your life.

_____

_____

_____

_____

_____

_____

_____

Identify one way money might have gained control over your life. What will you do to take control of that situation?

_____

_____

_____

_____

_____

On the one hand...

Indebtedness sometimes results from medical crises, loss of income due to job loss or death of a primary wage earner, something unexpected or out of your control. However, many times, indebtedness is the result of an unbridled desire for more, bigger, and better. It has often been noted, "Today, we are consumed with the desire to buy things we don't need, with money we don't have, to impress people we don't like." Often we are persuaded to buy that "deal that's too good to pass up" when in reality we should stop and think before we tack on more debt.

In what direction are you led when you consider Proverbs 22:7, which reads, "The rich rules over the poor, and **the borrower is servant to the lender**" (emp. added)? Are you interested in buying more "things" on credit or do you feel more motivated to pay off the debts you already have?

_____

_____

_____

_____

Link #3: *On a piece of paper write out two debts that you currently owe that could be paid off within a year if you limited excess spending. Post that piece of paper on the refrigerator or a highly visible area so that you are constantly reminded of this goal.*

On the other hand...

Sometimes the problem is not being enslaved to the monthly credit card bill. Rather, individuals sometimes have ample income to cover their monthly expenses – and then some! The problem is not in having too little; it is in having too much! The desire to accumulate more and More and MORE to the exclusion of God is a sin which many fall victim to in a world of unbridled prosperity. The "Almighty Dollar" becomes the heart's love and desire instead of The Almighty God. The pursuit of new money and new things leads to one's often unintended decision to serve Mammon. Money is an unrelenting taskmaster. It drives people to work for it, stretch for it, do things for it that they would never have thought of doing before. And then, when one's life and health are ruined because money was priority number one, the poor soul will go to the grave without even a penny to take with him.

Read the following passages:

Proverbs 1:19 "So are the ways of everyone who is **greedy for gain; It takes away the life of its owners.**"

Proverbs 23:4-5 **"Do not overwork to be rich;** Because of your own understanding, cease! Will you set your eyes on that which is not? For riches certainly make themselves wings; they fly away like an eagle toward heaven."

Proverbs 28:20 "A faithful man will abound with blessings, but **he who hastens to be rich will not go unpunished.**"

I Timothy 6:9-10 "But **those who desire to be rich** fall into temptation and a snare, and into many foolish and harmful lusts which drown men in destruction and perdition. For **the love of money** is a root of all kinds of evil, for which some have strayed from the faith in their greediness, and pierced themselves through with many sorrows."

Link #4: *On a piece of cardstock or heavy paper write down the name and address of three works of the church that you could give surplus income to and place the card in your wallet or money clip. And then follow through by giving to these works.*

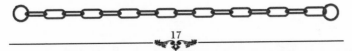

When you read the previous four scriptures, are you compelled to start down - or forge ahead on - a path of "unbridled accumulation"? Is the "one million dollar prize" that seems to be all the rage still a treasure to be coveted? Are you living a balanced life, or is your desire for the things of this world your motivation? What is your new attitude toward money?

_____

_____

_____

_____

_____

Read Job 31: 24-25, 28. Has money become your confidence? If so, realize the need to put your trust back in the One True God and put money in its proper place (Proverbs 3: 5-10).

For practical application please consider the example using credit cards found in Appendix A.

CHAPTER
TWO

Prosperity Theology

> SURPLUS WEALTH IS A SACRED TRUST
> WHICH ITS POSSESSOR IS BOUND TO
> ADMINISTER IN HIS LIFETIME FOR THE
> GOOD OF THE COMMUNITY.
> — American philanthropist, Andrew Carnegie

The September 18, 2006 *Time* magazine cover depicts a Rolls Royce complete with a crucifix as hood ornament and asks the question, "Does God Want You to be Rich?" Inside, the question is addressed and debated by a number of well-known protestant evangelists. The debate centers on the appropriateness of the so-called "Prosperity Gospel." As one might expect, the answers are varied and leave the impression that the Bible is too complicated to know for sure, so why not just let each decide for himself? Sounds eerily similar to the formula being used in Judges 17:6 and 21:25 ("everyone did what was right in his own eyes"), does it not?

But can we know the answer? Over the course of the next three chapters, let us explore God's Word and investigate three very different answers to the question, "Does God Want You to be Rich?" At the risk of ruining the suspense, let me assure you, two of the three answers are wrong!

Let's begin by considering this "theology of Prosperity." Sometimes referred to as **Name it and Claim it, Health and Wealth, or the Prosperity Gospel**, by any name this doctrine is neither good news nor The Good News! It is a theology that places too much value on the here and now, things, and temporal, earthly blessings. As a result it activates such heart problems as envy, covetousness, greed, and discontent.

> QUESTION: ARE MATERIAL POSSESSIONS
> A "SIGN" OF GOD'S APPROVAL?

Prosperity's promoters will turn to John 10:10 and quote Jesus, who said, "I have come that they may have life, and have it more abundantly." Or they will look to Matthew 7:7-8 and hone in on, "Ask and it will be given to you; seek, and you will find; knock, and it will be opened to you. For everyone who asks receives, and he who seeks finds, and to him who knocks it will be opened." Or maybe they will point out that it seems blessings come in return for giving according to Luke 6:38 or Malachi 3:10.

However, they will struggle with passages which seem to mitigate their stance. Like Matthew 6:19-21, which begins, "Do not lay up for yourselves treasures on earth, where moth and rust destroy and where thieves break in and steal…". Or Proverbs 23:4-5, "Do not overwork to be rich…". Or Revelation 3:17, "Because you say, 'I am rich, have become wealthy, and have need of nothing'—and do not know that you are wretched, miserable, poor, blind, and naked…" Purveyors of the gospel of Prosperity selectively disregard much of what the Bible teaches about finances.

Yet, according to the *Time* article, those who would defend the Prosperity gospel are adept at providing comparable book, chapter, and verse to silence its detractors. Maybe that's part of the problem. The Bible is not a collection of differing thoughts and ideologies. It is one book, composing one theme from cover to cover. Therefore, rather than pitting one verse against another, one must take it as a whole and discern the truth. The legitimacy of Psalm 119:160 is forever upheld, "The **sum** of your word is truth, and every one of your righteous rules endures forever."

Instead, proponents of Prosperity single out the verses that place a seeming emphasis on worldly wealth while steering clear of the verses that balance the view. They mistreat verses and hold them up as some sort of spiritual contract with God: a "give more to get more" philosophy that replaces God, the true and living God, with an almost mythological god who casts his favor toward those who would keep him appeased.

The problems with the Prosperity gospel are many. The danger in adopting this "other gospel" (Galatians 1:8) is that we no longer focus on eternal blessings and instead favor blessings which will not last. During the remainder of this chapter, let's consider some of the difficulties and counter them with God's Word.

Link #5: *In trying to get a handle on your personal finances, make sure that you maintain a proper sense of priorities by studying the Scriptures. It is easy to be misled if money is the central focus of your life.*

Harmful Seeds Sown by "Prosperity"

The Prosperity gospel tells its followers that God will *materially* bless one's *spiritual* faithfulness. It promotes the thought that the abundant life Christ referred to in John 10:10 is one of abundant material blessing while here on Earth. In effect, it says, "Aspire to achieve the American Dream of financial prosperity. God wants you to be financially rich and if you aren't, well, there's something wrong with you!"

Therefore, the necessary logical conclusion is that those who are not blessed financially must have something amiss in their spiritual lives. Or, they don't have enough faith. Similar thinking was employed by the Pharisees in the first century. Ironically, those same Pharisees turned up their noses (Luke 16:14) when Jesus taught the people that one could not serve both God and Mammon, for they were lovers of money.

The very purveyors of "freedom" through a life of financial prosperity are ultimately selling themselves and their followers into a life of bondage to the god of this fallen world. As they do, they are sowing seeds of discontent, covetousness, greed and envy. They install a "treadmill of American consumerism" in the hearts and minds of people. On this treadmill, the masses run and run and run trying to outspend, out consume, and "out new" their neighbors. While running, they think they are making progress and are better off for it, but they are actually worse for the wear – and truly going nowhere. Instead of nurturing a relationship with other people and with the living and true God, these souls become enslaved to the god of "just a little bit more," and hearts become covetous.

Link #6: *Satan is real. He knows our weaknesses and temptations. Where do you think Satan will attack you next? As faithful Christians, it is not enough to simply acknowledge His existence; we must also be prepared to counter temptation with spiritual discipline.*

Tommy "can't keep his eyes off" Calvin's new car. Calvin broods over Lori's new home. Lori "can't help" but feel a little green with envy when Katie walks by with her fancy new bag and shoes. Katie just "can't bring herself" to be happy about the land Tommy just bought. They all wonder, "Why can't I have that? After all, I'm a faithful Christian!"

Meanwhile, Larry has lost his job. Suzy lost a fortune in the stock market. Renee's washer and dryer went out – on the same day. And Ken's car is back in the shop. They all wonder, "Why can't I seem to get ahead? Why won't the Lord bless me? After all, I'm a faithful Christian!"

Every one of them has missed the point and been blinded to the truth because they bought into the deception that is the Prosperity gospel. And the seeds of discontent, covetousness, greed, and envy have grown like thorns and thistles such that "the cares of this world, the deceitfulness of riches, and the desires for other things entering in" (Mark 4:19) have managed to choke out the Truth of God's Word.

Beware the seeds of deception.

Link #7: *Write down two examples of the past in which you found yourself wanting to "keep up with the Joneses." Beside this write down two ways you can prevent such behavior in the future.*

Giving to Get

The Prosperity gospel also fosters a mindset where its followers begin to think of God as their own personal investment account (complete with ATM privileges!). The thought is a mutation of Luke 6:38, which reads, "Give and it will be given to you: good measure, pressed down, shaken together, and running over will be put into your bosom. For with the same measure that you use, it will be measured back to you." So is the verse true, or is it false? Of course it's true – it is God's inspired Word. But just like any other false doctrine, the Prosperity gospel takes a nugget of truth and morphs it into something ungodly.

As faithful Christians, we are called to give, ourselves first, then of our material blessings (2 Corinthians 8). Notice, we are not called to give "of" ourselves. We are to give our very lives to Christ. If we give "of" ourselves the implication is that we get to keep some of self (to meet our own purposes and fulfill our own desires). We must first give ourselves. This means our will must be shaped and molded to fit His will.

As we take on this mindset we will come to understand that we cannot out-give God (2 Corinthians 9:7-8; Philippians 4:18-19). God will reward us if we are faithful in steward-ship (Luke 19:12-24) not so that we can use it on our own whims, but so that we can continue to abound with even more generosity. Do you find yourself always lacking for time? Take inventory of how you currently use your time. Are you using it in ways which glorify God and strengthen yourself and others? If not, you may have uncovered why you don't *think* you have the time to give to help in the work of the Church. You should try it sometime; you cannot out-give God. He will supply the needs of those who are generous – whether it is in the giving of time, talent, or money.

However, the manner in which we approach the command to give of our means does make a difference. **Giving because of a sincere love for God, His church, our fellow man, and out of a generous heart is right and good but giving out of a desire to profit from our relationship with God is an improper motivation and heretical to the core.**

Link #8: *Take a minute to examine your heart. When you give to the church or faithful works, what is your true mindset toward letting that money go?*

May we reject any message which would lead our thinking astray and causes us to grow hearts which conform to a society that promotes materialism. May we instead give as we have been prospered. May we be motivated by the ultimate gift God gave in the person of His only begotten Son and the eternal hope available to His obedient children.

God's view of prosperity

Is there anyone out there who has read this chapter and is still thinking, "So which is it? Does He or does He not want me to be rich?" Friend, is that really the question which needs to be asked? Should we instead ask the question, "Why do I want to be rich?" Is it so you can use it for self, or is it so you can glorify God? **Whether or not you consider yourself to be rich, what are you doing right now with what you have?**

Simply put, God is **not** opposed to financial prosperity. It is He who gives us the power and ability to obtain wealth, according to Ecclesiastes 5:19. James 1:17 and 1 Timothy 6:17 which teach us that the blessings He provides come from Him and are given to us to enjoy. Wealth is good and proper when we understand we are but stewards or managers, not owners, for God owns all things.

Consider 1 Chronicles 29:11-16:

Yours, O Lord, is the greatness, the power and the glory, the victory and the majesty; For all that is in heaven and in earth is Yours; Yours is the kingdom, O Lord, and You are exalted as head over all.

Both riches and honor come from You, and You reign over all. In Your hand is power and might; In Your hand it is to make great and to give strength to all.

Now therefore, our God, we thank You And praise Your glorious name.

But who am I, and who are my people,

*that we should be able to offer so willingly as this? **For all things come from You, and of Your own we have given You.***

For we are aliens and pilgrims before You, as were all our fathers; Our days on earth are as a shadow, and without hope. O Lord our God, all this abundance that we have prepared to build You a house for Your holy name is from Your hand, and is all Your own.

He is, however, keenly aware of the slippery slope we encounter when we give ourselves over to the unbridled pursuit of "more." As such, throughout the Scripture, He has supplied us with myriad warnings regarding the pursuit of material gain. Proverbs 23:4 reads, "Do not toil to acquire wealth; be discerning enough to desist" (ESV). Proverbs 28:20 states, "A faithful man will abound with blessings, but he who hastens to be rich will not go unpunished." And Paul wrote to Timothy in 1 Timothy 6:7-10 that

> "…we brought nothing into this world, and it is certain we can carry nothing out. And having food and clothing, with these we shall be content. But those who desire to be rich fall into temptation and a snare, and into many foolish and harmful lusts which drown men in destruction and perdition. For the love of money is a root of all kinds of evil, for which some have strayed from the faith in their greediness, and pierced themselves through with many sorrows."

In the end, it matters not whether we are rich or poor - all will face the judgment without any money or material wealth to carry with us. Ultimately, our relationship with God will not be measured a success by the size of our bank account or estate. Rather, the relationship will be measured by the faithfulness with which we used that which He has given. From the parable of the talents found in Matthew 25:14-30, we learn that some are given to be stewards over much and some are to be stewards over little. Verse 15 clarifies why there is a difference. In the parable, each man was given "according to his ability." Likewise, for us today, God knows what we can handle. Jeremiah 17:10 reads, "I the Lord search the heart and test the mind, to give every man according to his ways, according to the fruit of his deeds." God will give us exactly what we need and exactly what we can handle, to serve Him exactly the way He wants. **The question for us is what are we doing with what He has given?**

Link #9: *Write a list of things you need in your life. Now review that list and identify those items that are actually "wants" instead of needs. Review the list one more time and ask yourself how strongly you "need" (can't live without) the items that remain. For those items still on the list, determine how you will pay for them. For those that don't make the list, come back to them in six months and see if you still "need" them.*

The Prosperity gospel is false doctrine. May we look to God's Word every day and learn the truth so that we can see clearly the repackaged lies that Satan sells. May we "let our conduct be without covetousness" and "be content with such things as we have" (Hebrews 13:5). In doing so we will then measure our prosperity not by our riches, but by the richness of our faith in "Jehovah-Jireh" (The-Lord-Will-Provide, Genesis 22:14).

Thoughts for discussion

What are some ways you have been influenced to live a life that follows the Prosperity gospel?

_____

_____

_____

When are some times you have been motivated to give to the church or to others in hopes of getting some material blessing in return?

_____

_____

_____

When you read Ecclesiastes 5:19 and 1 Chronicles 29:11-16 what happens to your understanding of God's view of material wealth?

_____

_____

_____

Is being wealthy sinful?

_____

_____

_____

Is it the wealth or the faithfulness with which we distribute
the wealth that interests God the most? Is it the wealth or
the trust we place in wealth instead of God that is the sin?
Read 1 Timothy 6:17 and Proverbs 11:4.

_____

_____

_____

Would you consider adding the thoughts of this prayer to
your daily prayer life?

Father in heaven, Giver of all good things, may I understand
my role *and* **money's role** *in Your will and* **Your kingdom.**
May I look into Your Word and learn to view money and
wealth as **You** *see them. May I then do my part to apply*
what I've learned. May I never give out of motivation to get
more so that I can spend it on myself. May I instead have a
heart that is willing to give more so that when You give me
more, I will have even more to give to others. I know that
then **You** *will be glorified. May I be a willing participant in*
giving **You** *the glory that is Yours. In Jesus' name, Amen.*

CHAPTER
THREE

Poverty Theology

> POVERTY IS NO DISGRACE TO A MAN, BUT
> IT IS CONFOUNDEDLY INCONVENIENT.
> – English writer, Sydney Smith

"Does God want me to be... poor?"

Is it wrong for someone to have wealth? Is it more spiritual, more morally excellent – more righteous – to voluntarily forego material things? Should one feel guilty if he or she finds a level of enjoyment in having "this world's goods?" Would God have everyone sell all that he has and distribute to the poor? What exactly is *asceticism* anyway?

In chapter 2 we looked into a false doctrine know by many as "the Prosperity Gospel." We considered its tempting appeal. We noticed its many shortcomings and misapplication of Scripture. We acknowledged that it is not gospel – in fact, it's just the opposite – *it's bad news*!

So then should we swing to the opposite side? If, in fact, the Prosperity gospel is wrong would it be better for us to subscribe to a Poverty theology instead? Let's consider the doctrine, its logical conclusions, and its consequences to see what we may determine.

Asceticism is the belief that wealth is wrong. Poverty is held up as the way we can set ourselves apart from the world (worldliness). While purveyors of Prosperity teach that faithfulness to God is evidenced by financial abundance and vice versa, and ultimately find themselves like Belshazzar and company praising the gods of gold and silver, bronze and iron, wood and stone (Daniel 5:1-4), those espousing Poverty swerve to the other side of the issue by abhorring anything (and often, anyone) whom they perceive to be rich with this world's goods. In a culture of materialism and worldliness, "taking the other side" may seem like the thing to do. Maybe asceticism is the prescription that will get people off the treadmill of American consumerism!

Link #10: *As you enter your church building this week, consider what would happen if everyone you greeted decided to subscribe to Poverty theology. Take a minute to discern what would happen with evangelism, mission work, and benevolence at your local congregation.*

Many Christians struggle between the two extremes of Poverty and Prosperity. On the one hand, they point to the latter part of 1 Timothy 6:17 ("…God, who gives us richly all things to enjoy") and believe that God blesses materially and that all good things come from Him (James 1:17). On the other hand, they feel guilty about having material wealth and its attendant blessings because they "think of all the people who have little or nothing," they hear Jesus' words to the rich young ruler telling them to "sell all and give to the poor" (Luke 18:22), and they read *into* 1 Timothy 6:10 that money is the root of all evil.

What are we as Christians to do? Is there a way to understand and get to the truth of the matter? In the balance of this chapter, let's consider what God's Word has to say on the topic and address these questions:

1. Are possessions wrong?
2. Is money really the root of all evil?
3. What are the consequences of all Christians giving up "this world's goods"?

Are Possessions Wrong?
Renouncing material possessions is one of the major tenets of Poverty theology. But is it a biblical practice?

With only a little time spent in either the Old or the New Testament, one will shatter the notion that having possessions is wrong. From the patriarchs like Abraham, Isaac, Jacob, and Job - to Israel's and Judah's kings like David, Solomon, Hezekiah, and Jehoshapahat - to first century examples like Zaccheus, Joseph of Arimathea, and Lydia the Bible is replete with examples of faithful men and women who were also materially blessed. Throughout Psalms, Proverbs, and Ecclesiastes, the principles of faithful sowing and plentiful reaping are found.

So what's the problem? The problem arises with the **improper use** of possessions. The problem is found in the heart. The problem is found in our attitude, approach, and motivation for attaining material wealth. Our lusts for things, covetousness for more, envy of others, and entanglement with worldly pursuits is the sin. It is the attitude of heart that dictates whether having possessions is good or bad. So, rather than focus on the externals by removing things (possessions) from our lives, God would have us cleanse our hearts of the iniquity of idolatry (Colossians 3:5; 2 Peter 2:14; 1 John 2:15-17) and **properly manage** the blessings He provides.

Link #11: *In countries outside of the United States people are often very generous. Consider some of your "prized possessions." Could you give them away to someone right now if you knew it would make their life better?*

Is Money really the root of all evil?

"But those who desire to be rich fall into temptation and a snare, and into many foolish and harmful lusts which drown men in destruction and perdition. For the love of money is a root of all kinds of evil, for which some have strayed from the faith in their greediness, and pierced themselves through with many sorrows."
(1 Timothy 6:9-10)

The answer to the question previously asked: No, *money* is not the root of all evil.

But, the *love* of money is a root of all kinds of evil. It's not the money but the love of the money that is the problem. It's not money itself but the love of it – and our attitude toward it – that is the root from which all kinds of evil can spring forth. One may be rich and love money. *But, one may be poor and love money too*. The rich person may see the good that can come from having material blessings and desire more good. He may find himself trusting in riches rather than God. He may hoard money in a vain attempt at security, stray from the faith as a result, and pierce himself through with many sorrows stemming from greediness (vs. 10). Or, one may lack material wealth, see the pleasures others enjoy, and commit soul and self to the pursuit of this world's goods. In the lust and desire to be rich, one may willingly forfeit the treasures of eternity for a piece of today's good life. Ultimately, the love of money will consume his thoughts and actions and cause him to pursue money in unethical and sinful ways (vs. 9).

Link #12: *How much do your children love money? Have they grown up in an environment where money is a central focus, or is it simply a tool to obtain the goods needed for the family? Consider having a home devotional this week on the topic of money and greed.*

Hebrews 13:5 admonishes us to "keep [our lives] free from the love of money, and be content with what [we] have… (ESV). Is being rich the problem? No. It is nurturing the desire to be rich rather than fostering contentment that causes the sin. It is the lust for money that gives birth to sin (James 1:15).

Rather than eschew all things material (particularly money) as Poverty theology dictates, we would do better to "remember the Lord [our] God, for it is He who gives [us] the power to get wealth" (Deuteronomy 8:18). It is all His (Psalm 24:1; Job 41:11, et al.). We are keepers of that which is His (1 Corinthians 4:2; Romans 14:10, 12). And, we are to glorify Him in all that we do – including the way we make use of money (2 Corinthians 8:7; 9:10-13). Pause right now and spend some time in 2 Corinthians 8 and 9. Get to know your brethren from first century Macedonia. They will help us understand what God expects of us.

What are the consequences of all Christians giving up "this world's goods"?

Consider the admonitions found in Luke 6:38, 2 Corinthians 9:7-8, and Proverbs 3:9-10. If, as Christians, we attempt to live a fully ascetic lifestyle, we must first get rid of everything material that we have. Then, we must not have anything to do with a mechanism that would potentially increase our wealth (i.e., a job). Thus, we would out of necessity likely need to reside somewhere communal while depending on the goodwill of others (who are heathens by the very definition of Poverty theology) and the forced redistribution of wealth to provide for our physical needs.

> QUESTION: IF WE HAVE NOTHING HOW ARE WE TO FULFILL THE COMMANDS TO GIVE?

The fact is that, as a part of His divine providence God has entrusted each accountable person with the ability to prosper to some degree. As Christians we may not be the wealthiest people and we likely will not be the poorest people. It is our duty to work, to earn a wage, and to provide for our needs and the needs of those *unable* to provide for themselves. We are to do this - we can only do this – by not going to the extremes of Poverty theology.

Conclusion

The danger in espousing extremes is that in doing so we wind up adding to or taking away from God's direction for our lives. When we do this, we inadvertently substitute our will and wisdom for God's will and wisdom. At least three times in the book of Deuteronomy, the people are admonished to **turn aside to neither the right hand or the left** but to **walk in *all* the ways the Lord God has commanded** (Deuteronomy 5:32; 17:20; 28:14, emp. added). The rationale behind the warning was that through obedience to God it would be well with the people, their days would be prolonged in the land which they possessed, and so they would not go after other gods.

In order for us to walk in all the ways the Lord God has commanded we must train our hearts and minds with thorough application of all of God's Word. We must prepare our hearts to willingly accept God's provision and use it to His glory. That way we will not be enamored with and deluded by extremes that would endanger our souls and the souls of others. Rather, we will then begin to have the attitude of the writer of Proverbs 30:8-9 which reads, "Remove falsehood and lies far from me; **give me neither poverty nor riches** – feed me with the food allotted to me; lest I be full and deny You, and say, 'Who is the Lord?' or lest I be poor and steal, and profane the name of my God" (emp. added).

Link #13: *In balancing your family budget, how often do you meditate on Scriptures for insight and wisdom? How often do you begin your prayers with thanksgiving for all He has given compared to "Lord, I really need...?" Do you routinely ask God for His blessings and His counsel on what to do with His blessings?*

Thoughts for discussion

Are possessions wrong? Proverbs 21:20; Proverbs 22:4

_____

_____

_____

Is money the root of all evil? 1 Timothy 6:9-10; Hebrews 13:5 (ESV) If not, what is?

_____

_____

_____

What are the consequences of all Christians giving up "this world's goods"?

_____

_____

_____

Instead of forsaking all things material what should we do instead as managers of His estate?

Read Matthew 25:14-30, Luke 16:10-13, Deuteronomy 15:11, and Proverbs 3:9.

_____

_____

_____

_____

CHAPTER
FOUR

STEWARDSHIP THEOLOGY

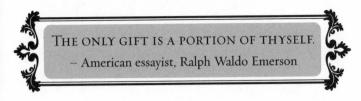

THE ONLY GIFT IS A PORTION OF THYSELF.
— American essayist, Ralph Waldo Emerson

What does God want from me?

"Shall I come before Him with burnt offerings, with calves a year old? Will the Lord be pleased with thousands of rams, ten thousand rivers of oil? Shall I give my firstborn for my transgression, the fruit of my body for the sin of my soul?" (Micah 6:6-7)

Micah asks the rhetorical question: Can I ever give enough to please or satisfy my God? Is there anything I can give that will compare to what God gave in the person of His only begotten Son? The answers are a resounding "no" and "nothing" respectively.

However, in Micah 6:8 the Lord Himself reveals what **He wants. He wants us to do justly, to love mercy, and to walk humbly with Him**. In Deuteronomy 10:12-14, after reviewing the commandments with Israel, Moses summarized what God expected by saying, "what does the Lord your God require of you, but to fear the Lord your God, to walk in all His ways and to love Him, to serve the Lord your God with all your heart and with all your soul, and to keep the commandments of the Lord and His statutes which I command you today for your good? Indeed heaven and the highest heavens belong to the Lord your God, also the earth and all that is in it."

God owns everything, even the material things of this world. He provides for our needs and gives to us for our good. He wants us to obey Him and walk with Him – even in the area of our finances. Obeying our God in all areas of our lives will be for our own good. Are you beginning to see why Faith and Finance are inseparably linked?

The last two chapters have addressed two questions that seem to trouble the Christian: ***Does God want me to be rich? Or does God want me to be poor?*** After considering the virtues and consequences of each viewpoint – each theology – hopefully you have come away with the understanding that an unqualified yes to either question is an inappropriate response. Hopefully, you are wondering if the questions themselves are even appropriate! My prayer is that you have come away convinced that some virtues upheld by each viewpoint are interwoven in the Truth of God's Word and when taken along with the rest – the whole counsel of God – we can find our balance. **I can then understand what God wants: He wants me to be faithful.**

Link #14: *Faith and Finances are inseparably linked! Evaluate the areas of faith and finance in your life. Where can you do better?*

Ultimately, our eternal destiny is not dependent upon our accumulation – or avoidance – of earthly, material, or financial assets. God is not interested in the appraisal of our real estate, the balance in our checking or savings accounts, the value of our investment portfolio, or even the calculation of our net worth. Remember it is all His already. **God is most interested in our hearts, our attitudes, our motivations and the resulting manner in which we *view* financial blessings and *use* them.** Of course, our financial statement – one that shows "riches kept for their owner to his hurt" (Ecclesiastes 5:13) or one that reveals servitude to debt (Proverbs 22:7) – could indicate an underlying heart problem. But, the underlying heart problem is what needs to be diagnosed and remedied. Here is the key: the required diagnosis comes from a **self examination** under the light of God's Word.

It is unlikely that any of us could diagnose a Christian with a financial heart problem unless we get to know that Christian very well. Over time, the fruit of one's life may well give a strong indication one way or the other. But we should be careful, as appearances can be deceiving. We may very well think that someone *looks* materialistic when in fact he gives 50, 60, 70, 80% or more of his income to God and His causes – but because he is so materially blessed he still has nice things we determine he is materialistic.

Link #15: *Far too often homes today are cluttered with hundreds of toys and video games. Houses continue to grow and storage sheds are rented to house all of our "stuff." What are some real gifts we can give our children that will help them when it comes to faith and finances?*

On the other hand, people may look like they have little. They may not drive new cars, or own large houses, or wear new clothes – but they die and it is revealed that their estate is worth millions. Did they trust in God or in the value of their estate? Could they not find it in their hearts to give while they were alive? Were they afraid they would "go broke" therefore lived as misers to keep that from happening? No one can know for sure, except for God. **But, please realize, God does know how we are managing the blessings He's provided. He knows our hearts and He knows who is faithful. God is not fooled by our appearances (I Samuel 16:7).**

Let's spend the next few minutes doing a self examination by shining His light on our lives.

God's Word says God Wants My Best

"Well done, good and faithful servant; you have been faithful over a few things…"
"He who is faithful in what is least is faithful also in much…"
"And whatever you do, do it heartily as to the Lord and not to men…"

In the famous parable of the talents, we read that the master at his own discretion gave to "each according to his ability." The servants were then to make use of the talents to produce more talents. Those who did so were rewarded as faithful. Likewise we are required, as faithful stewards, to do our best, be our best, and make the most out of the gifts He supplies – however much, or little, we may have.

One who aspires to live a life of faithful stewardship makes the decision that while using biblical principles, he will faithfully manage and administer the gifts God has provided. This means he will throw off any self image of either significance *or* insignificance and get busy working for God to serve His purpose.

Like Gideon of old, many today have a poor self image and as a result fall short of the good they could be doing. They know their weaknesses and compare themselves with others. Instead of recognizing they have innate value as a child of the Creator and Sustainer they, like Gideon, proclaim, "My family history is one of weakness, and I am the weakest and most unworthy of them all!" Please understand God's disappointment when His creation chooses to see only the problems and weaknesses in their lives rather the bountiful good He has supplied!

Others may swell with pride when they consider all they have. They may give out of improper motivation in an effort to feel superior to others who can't give as high of a dollar amount. They enjoy their "status" and "standing" as significant givers when in reality they may be holding out on God (see Acts 5).

As faithful stewards we also will recognize the abilities God has entrusted into our care. In other words, if we have the ability to produce large sums of income ethically and while keeping God first place in life, then by all means labor in the vocation that allows for that particular income level. On the other hand, if our skill set does not lend itself to what we believe is a "substantial" income, we must still do our best and provide the first fruits back to God. In all that we do, we should always strive to accomplish our best and never shy away from whatever our abilities allow us to achieve.

Let us resolve to acknowledge that God is bigger than any difficulty, challenge, or weakness we face and let us stop fretting over whether or not we will have what we need. He has always provided for His people. As Christians we would do well to measure our days not by the harvest we bring in but by the seeds we sow. It is the seeds that we sow together – individual members doing what each one can do – that will make the difference. God requires us to offer Him our best by consistently doing our best. We **can** do better.

Link #16: *In acknowledging that God is bigger than anything we may face, what are some Scriptures you can refer back to that speak of the power and might of our Creator?*

God's Word says God Wants My Best, (part 2)
So, what does it mean to be rich? Does buying a $300,000 house make one rich financially? Ask a family struggling to find a $300,000 house in southern California if they consider themselves rich. And what does it mean to be poor? According to the Department of Health and Human Services, the "poverty line" for a family of four living in the United States is an annual income of approximately $20,000. Would $20,000 not be quite a windfall in a third world country?

The point is that attempting to measure our wealth with dollar figures is a very subjective practice. In fact, God does not measure our prosperity in dollars. Rather than focus our efforts on determining whether our neighbors are rich or poor and rather than spending our time comparing ourselves with others, let us ensure that as individuals we are exercising faithful stewardship.

Find – and Keep – Your Balance

God's faithful steward leads a life of balance. One living a balanced life is one that realizes that it is acceptable to enjoy the bountiful blessings that come from a life of utilizing one's talents to the fullest. One living in balance also understands the divine responsibility to support the work of the Church and provide for the needs of others.

Link #17: *Name just one thing you can do to help improve your faith and finance situation. Now, write down the steps it will take to get that accomplished…and start today to get it done.*

The proper perspective with regard to handling monetary blessings (our personal finances) is one of stewardship. We must understand our roles as stewards of the blessings of God. Should a Christian be rich? Absolutely – rich toward God! Someone once said, "A lot of people are willing to give God the credit, but not too many are willing to give Him the cash." If we follow that line of thinking we do not understand that God *will* ultimately be given the credit. **He will be glorified when we stop serving money and start serving God with our money – by becoming generous stewards.**

As you examine yourself and consider the way you handle the financial blessings you have gained by obediently laboring, consider the following golf analogy. I have heard it said that when holding a golf club we should treat the grip as if it were a small bird. We must hold on tightly enough that the bird does not squirm free and fly away. Contrarily, we must not hold on too tightly and crush and kill the bird. So it goes with money. Faithful stewardship requires that we exercise discretion when making financial decisions (both large and small). On the one hand it means not wasting our blessings. And on the other hand, it means not holding on so tightly and miserly that we die with money in our bank accounts and estates that should have already been contributed to the Lord's work or used to provide for our families.

You see, as Christians we must understand our role as stewards, or managers, of God's gifts. We may choose to hoard them up to our detriment (e.g., the rich fool in Luke 12:15-21) or become greedy for gain. In doing so we forfeit our lives (Proverbs 1:19). Or, we may choose to shun *all forms* of material blessings (including the industrious sowing [think, a job] that would lead to reaping a financial harvest). Then we would become a burden to others because of our "righteousness" - despite scriptural direction to the contrary (Proverbs 22:4; Ephesians 4:28; Deuteronomy 8:18). Or we may choose the right way - God's way. If we determine to serve God (and not Mammon) as Lord of our lives, then we would:

- excel with the talents and abilities God has given us (Matthew 25:15ff)
- be industrious and seek ways to work effectively with our skill set (Proverbs 6:6-8; 14:23)
- trust God to always give us what we need even when we can't see how we could possibly make it (Hebrews 11:1; Philippians 4:13)
- keep Him first even in financial decisions (Matthew 6:33; Philippians 2:21)
- provide for the needs of others (Psalm 112:9a; Proverbs 21:26b)
- support the work of the Church (2 Corinthians 8:1-8; 9:6-9)
- glorify God in our hearts by our faithful actions (1 Timothy 6:17-19; 2 Corinthians 9:12-14)

The Bible is clear in teaching that the Lord wants what is best for each of us both now and in eternity. When we have prepared the right heart and mind to receive God's blessings of prosperity, whether financially, intellectually, physically, or spiritually, the increase God gives will then be used by us to further glorify Him. If we have properly cultivated a generous heart, we will, with all of our blessings: do justly, love mercy, and walk humbly with our God. He will be glorified both in the life of those who receive our good gifts and in our own lives as cheerful givers. **Successful stewardship is using what you have to do the most good you can**. Let us resolve to be faithful stewards starting today!

Link #18: *Name one talent you could better utilize for God. Have a family devotional in which everyone identifies their talents and ways they can be used to further His kingdom. Put those plans into action.*

Thoughts for discussion

What kind of steward have you been so far? Have you been a faithful manager over the gifts God has given? Check your records for the last three months. Do the decisions you made match with the intentions you had? Remember, God knows your heart.

_____

_____

_____

Do you give generously? Do you consider yourself as one who gives a tithe? Do you give at all? Explain your answer.

_____

_____

_____

For practical application, please turn to Appendix B & C and complete the exercises found there.

I challenge you to take the thoughts contained in this prayer and incorporate them into your daily prayer life.

Dear Lord and father in heaven, I pray that my life's pursuit will be a pursuit of You and that I will resist the temptation to pursue wealth. I pray that I will draw closer to You each day and not be led astray by doctrines that would serve to separate me from You. May I embrace each day and each blessing as a gift (from You) to be used to glorify You. I pray that I will give you my best in every aspect of life. I pray that I will find balance in my understanding of money and wealth by knowing that You will supply my every need... May I be a faithful steward of what You give me – and use it to further Your kingdom, to care for my family's needs and the needs of others, and to provide a life for myself that is pleasing before you. May my faithful stewardship serve to bring glory not to me but You. In Jesus' name, Amen.

CHAPTER
FIVE

You Can't Take It With You

> WE MAKE A LIVING BY WHAT WE GET;
> WE MAKE A LIFE BY WHAT WE GIVE.
> – Prime Minister of the UK, Sir Winston Churchill

What does the title of a Hollywood movie voted Best Picture in the 1930's have to do with Faith and Finances in the 21st century? It serves as fitting reminder for how the Christian should view money and its friends. In a world which promotes money as a god: comforting, empowering, fulfilling, and esteem-boosting it is helpful to be reminded of the truth about wealth. For all the good it can do, money should never be elevated to the status of a god. The movie "You Can't Take it With You," voted best picture in 1938, reminds us of money's greatest weakness.

You Can't Take it with You
Though John D. Rockefeller was one of the wealthiest men of his day and a noted philanthropist, he died and was buried just like anyone else. Randy Alcorn, in his excellent book on stewardship, *The Treasure Principle*, tells the story that there was much interest about Rockefeller's will and estate. Someone inquired of his accountant, "How much money did John D. leave?" The reply was simple. "He left... all of it."

How much did Andrew Carnegie, Howard Hughes, and William Randolph Hearst leave? How much will Donald Trump, Bill Gates, Warren Buffet, and you and I leave? ALL of it.

Oh, but you say, "I am not rich." Wrong. Every American reading these words is, in fact, rich. While you may not realize that you are it does not change the fact that you are. It is time for us to open our eyes to the Truth. **We have been blessed in abundance**. Whether we *feel* rich or *think* we are rich when we compare ourselves to those on the latest Forbes list is immaterial. Whether you feel rich or not, what you do have… You can't take it with you.

Despite our knowledge of this fact, we all too often behave as if it were only theory. The Bible makes it clear that there is no escaping the end result of our earthly lives.

"When one becomes rich, when the glory of his house is increased; …when he dies he shall carry nothing away. His glory shall not descend after him." (Psalm 49:16-17)

"But God said to him, 'Fool! This night your soul will be required of you; then whose will those things be which you have provided?'" (Luke 12:20)

"As he came from his mother's womb, naked shall he return, to go as he came; and he shall take nothing from his labor which he may carry in his hand." (Ecclesiastes 5:15)

If your purpose and plan is to work, spend, save, invest, and accumulate until you retire or die, your plan is "holey." That's right, it is full of holes. All of your effort is in vain. Call it the "Rich Fool Plan" (Luke 12:15-21). "*So is he* who lays up treasure for himself and is not rich toward God" (verse 21, emp. added). Are you living your life like the "he" mentioned in Luke 12:21? This short life, be it 50, 70, 90, or even 110 years, is vanity if it is spent accumulating treasure that is worthless in the "new heaven and new earth" (2 Peter 3:13). Colonel Sanders got it right when he said, "There's no need being the richest man in the cemetery. You can't do any business from there."

Link #19: *Fathers and mothers, what would it take in order for you to spend one more hour each week with your children? If you knew it would make your child happier and healthier would you be willing to make that sacrifice?*
Hint: It will make them happier and healthier.

We must reconsider our concept of money, wealth, and materialism. The world's mold into which we are constantly squeezed teaches us to value short term pleasure over long term gain. Society today would have us scoff at Moses as foolish for having given up Egypt's treasures (Hebrews

11:23-27). Our culture would have us ridicule Abram for not looking out for "number one" when Abram let Lot choose first (Genesis 13). And today's generation would likely suggest we question Paul's sanity for forsaking his pedigree in favor of Christ (Philippians 3:4-11).

Shouldn't we be busily wearying and worrying ourselves over protecting our "piece of the pie?" It is true that we have been given so much. We must exercise good, faithful stewardship over what we have been given. Some have seen their businesses flourish resulting in their being counted among the world's most prosperous (living in America, this part is easy). But, what are we doing with our increase – our abundance – that is, the amount above and beyond that which sustains our needs and those of our family? Will our money go with us when we die? Will we pass it on to our children and potentially harm them in doing so? Will we leave it to good causes through means of a will? Will we die with *God's money* in our bank accounts?

Conventional wisdom dictates that we follow the proper legal methods to establish a distribution plan for our estate in the event of our death. In other words, having a will is good and proper. As a result of uncertainty surrounding the exact date of our departure, leaving monies to the Church and good works is certainly appropriate. However, it is what we do with what God has entrusted us while we are living that requires the greatest discipline, wisdom, and godly encouragement. Because, you can't take it with you.

So what are we to do?

In the aforementioned book, *The Treasure Principle*, Alcorn puts it this way:

> "You can't take it with you – but you can send it on ahead."

Is this a biblical concept?

Consider the following passages, apply reasoning, and I believe you will conclude, as I do, that it is indeed biblical. First, in Philippians 4:17 Paul writes concerning the Philippians' generosity, "Not that I seek the gift, but I seek the fruit that *increases to your credit*" (ESV, **emp. added**). Or, "…I seek the profit that accrues to your account." Next, consider Paul's Spirit-led instructions to those who are rich that they not "trust in uncertain riches but in the living God who gives us richly all things to enjoy. Let them do good, that they be rich in good works, ready to give, ready to share, *storing up for themselves a good foundation for the time to come*, that they may lay hold on eternal life" (1 Timothy 6:17-19, **emp. added**). Finally, recall Jesus' words in Matthew 6:19-21, which read, "Do not lay up for yourselves treasures on earth, where moth and rust destroy and where thieves break in and steal; but lay up for yourselves treasures in heaven, where neither moth nor rust destroys and where thieves do not break in and steal. For where your treasure is, there your heart will be also."

Link #20: *What is one way that you personally could send your "treasure" ahead? Have you taken steps to ensure this becomes a reality?*

In the stock market, we invest in companies we are interested in or think will provide a high return. Maybe we invest in a new venture because a friend we trust is starting a business with a plan in which we believe. Are you willing to "buy into" the concept of Christ and the work of His church? Would you be interested in "investing" in significant, guaranteed returns that will never diminish in value and support a cause that has eternal benefits to yourself and others? You can invest in heavenly treasure today by the manner in which you spend or give the money you have.

Protestant preacher, A.W. Tozer put it this way:

"As base a thing as money often is, it yet can be transmuted into everlasting treasure. It can be converted into food for the hungry and clothing for the poor; it can keep a missionary actively winning lost men to the light of the gospel and thus transmute itself into heavenly values. Any temporal possession can be turned into everlasting wealth. Whatever is given to Christ is immediately touched with immortality."

What we do with our finances holds implications for both now and eternity. We must understand the fact that **faith and finances are inseparably linked**. When we speak of one, we are implying something about the other. What we do with one significantly affects the other. When you say you have faith, I can say, "Show me by what you do with your finances." If you say, "Look at the many ways God has blessed me," I should be able to assume you have, in turn, been a blessing in the lives of others by passing the blessings along. It should not be uncommon for Christians to give until they think it might hurt – only to have God supply their needs in abundance so they can increase their generosity even more. Faith and finance can no longer be kept in tidy compartments separated from one another (never could, really). **They must be separated no more.**

The choice is yours and mine and it is for today. *The here and now choice* is this: will we use the blessings we receive from God (Deuteronomy 8:18) to serve His purposes by contributing abundantly to the work of the Church, to missionaries, to benevolent outreach, and to taking the Gospel into all the world or will we spend most of it on ourselves in an attempt to meet worldly standards of excellence? *The eternal choice* is: will we invest in treasures that are nice for now but worthless in eternity, or will we increase our heavenly treasures by increasing our giving to fund the work of Christ and His church?

If your time on Earth ended today, how would your heavenly account compare to your earthly one? How much heavenly treasure have you laid up for eternity? Start today to build a portfolio that will last for eternity. You can begin today *truly* investing for the future in treasure that will never grow old, be destroyed, suffer market risk, or lose value.

Remember, while you can't take it with you, you can send it on ahead (voted best investment plan for all times by the Lord Himself).

Link #21: *Evaluate your beliefs on money before you sat down to read this book compared to now. In what areas can you make permanent changes to ensure that your faith and finances remain inseparably linked?*

Thoughts for discussion

1. Explain why Christians should save money and not give away *all* of the surplus with which they have been blessed. Read Proverbs 6:6-8, 13:22, and Genesis 41:33-49.

_____

_____

_____

_____

2. Is there a way to find balance between hoarding (keeping more than we need) with saving and investing for the future, along with ensuring our faithful distribution to the causes of Christ and His church? The following verses provide guidelines to do just that:

Luke 12:30-31 _____

1 Timothy 6:17-19_____

Philippians 4:17_____

2 Corinthians 8:5_____

2 Corinthians 8:7 _____

2 Corinthians 8:12-14 _____

3. With a good understanding, outlook, and attitude shouldn't we be more likely to "hold on loosely" to the material wealth that looks so attractive today? Does understanding that today's material wealth perishes but can be used to store up treasures in heaven motivate you to start a new kind of "eternal investment plan"? Describe the ways you will begin investing in eternity:

_____

_____

_____

_____

_____

_____

Consider taking the challenge implied by your filling your name in the blanks of the following pledge.

I pledge that I, _____, will begin today to put my faith and trust in Jehovah Jireh (The Lord will provide). I now understand that I cannot out give God. I realize that He owns all things and has committed some of this abundance into my hands to manage. It is not mine. I am a caretaker and steward. He has given me this wealth to supply my needs and the needs of my family. I realize He expects me to keep Him first in all that I do – including the giving of my finances – trusting Him to supply for my needs.

I pledge to put God first and keep Him first. I will expand the borders of my generosity beginning today. I pledge to increase my giving percentage from _____% to _____% so that I will be more helpful to even more people in need of food, clothing, shelter, medicine, and most of all, the Good News that will provide them with Eternal prosperity in heaven. In my obedience, I believe God's promise that He will take care of me.

I, _____, pledge to give my best on the job, not because I want the glory, but because in doing so I will honor God and He will get the glory. If and when I get an increase in my income, I pledge to give the firstfruits back to Him just like the faithful patriarchs of the Old Testament.

I am going to pursue an investment plan that will provide for my future needs. That is, I am going to be motivated not only because of a sense of duty to my God to do what is right but also because there is long term – yes, even eternal – benefit to laying up treasures in heaven. I want to experience the abundant heavenly retirement God has promised to those who are faithful in money matters.

I believe the sum of God's Word is truth and will faithfully live a life that is according to His purpose and His plan.

Appendix A:

Consider the credit card debt that currently owns you.
What is the true cost of paying only the minimum?
You can plug in the numbers specific to your situation at
www.bankrate.com.

Example

Credit card balance: **$5000**
Interest rate: **18%**
Monthly Minimum Percentage Payment: **2.5%** of outstanding balance*

*meaning you would pay $125 in month one [$5000 x .025 = $125] and that dollar amount declines as your outstanding balance declines

If you cut up the card today and charge nothing else but determine to pay it off by paying only the monthly minimum, it would take **313 months** (a little over *26 years and $7115 in interest charges later*) to pay it off.

However, if instead of paying the issuer's calculated monthly minimum each month, you paid a fixed amount of **$200 monthly**, you could have the card paid off in **32 months** (**under 3 years** and with *only* **$1313** in interest charges).

Consider, is a 30% off deal really a bargain when you end up paying twice as much for the item (in interest charges)?

Appendix B

Use the following charts to determine what percentage of your income you currently give.

To read the chart on the next page, start by finding your approximate annual income on the left side. The amount reported to you on your W2 might be a good starting point.

Then, moving left to right, find the amount you contributed to the work of the Church and other good works of benevolence, missions, etc. The percentage you gave is the column heading above the amount you determined.

What percentage are you giving each year?

_____

For example, say you made $50,000 last year, and you determine you gave $7500 to the work of the Church. Great! You gave 15% of your income to God and His causes.

Do you trust God enough to move up to 20% this year? Remember He promised to supply all your needs so you can help supply the needs of others!

Consider, if someone gave you a dollar and then asked for twenty cents back, what would you have? You'd have eighty cents more than you had before they gave it to you! Would you willingly begrudge God the same percentage, or even more? He's given you so very much.

Annual Analysis

Income	1%	5%	10%	15%	20%	30%	40%	50%
10000	100	500	1000	1500	2000	3000	4000	5000
12000	120	600	1200	1800	2400	3600	4800	6000
15000	150	750	1500	2250	3000	4500	6000	7500
18000	180	900	1800	2700	3600	5400	7200	9000
20000	200	1000	2000	3000	4000	6000	8000	10000
24000	240	1200	2400	3600	4800	7200	9600	12000
30000	300	1500	3000	4500	6000	9000	12000	15000
40000	400	2000	4000	6000	8000	12000	16000	20000
50000	500	2500	5000	7500	10000	15000	20000	25000
60000	600	3000	6000	9000	12000	18000	24000	30000
70000	700	3500	7000	10500	14000	21000	28000	35000
80000	800	4000	8000	12000	16000	24000	32000	40000
90000	900	4500	9000	13500	18000	27000	36000	45000
100000	1000	5000	10000	15000	20000	30000	40000	50000
120000	1200	6000	12000	18000	24000	36000	48000	60000
150000	1500	7500	15000	22500	30000	45000	60000	75000
180000	1800	9000	18000	27000	36000	54000	72000	90000
200000	2000	10000	20000	30000	40000	60000	80000	100000
300000	3000	15000	30000	45000	60000	90000	120000	150000
400000	4000	20000	40000	60000	80000	120000	160000	200000
500000	5000	25000	50000	75000	100000	150000	200000	250000

Appendix C

Maybe you would prefer to look at the numbers on a weekly basis. You say, "I know how much I make each year, and I know how much I give each week. Can you tell me what percentage I'm giving?" The answer is, "Yes."

Look at the chart on the next page. Using the same methodology as in appendix B, find your annual income on the left side. Then, moving left to right, find the approximate amount you give each week. The column heading is the percentage you give.

What percentage are you giving weekly?

For example, let's say you had a really good year and made $100,000. And, let's say you write a check for $150 to the Church where you attend each week. You do not currently give to other worthy causes but depend on the local Church to distribute your funds according to the leadership's decisions. Find $100,000 on the left side and then notice that the closest figure to $150 is the $192.31 under the 10% column. What can you conclude? You can conclude that the $150 check you write each week is not quite 10%.

Can you do better? Do you not want to do better?

God gave His best to us through His Son, Jesus. Does He not deserve our first and best?

Would you be willing to "go out on a limb," trust God to supply your needs, and begin giving a higher percentage to God first?

Weekly Analysis

Income	1%	5%	10%	15%	20%	30%	40%	50%
10000	1.92	9.62	19.23	28.8	38.46	200.00	76.92	96.15
12000	2.31	11.54	23.08	34.6	46.15	240.00	92.31	115.38
15000	2.88	14.42	28.85	43.3	57.69	300.00	115.38	144.23
18000	3.46	17.31	34.62	51.9	69.23	360.00	138.46	173.08
20000	3.85	19.23	38.46	57.7	76.92	400.00	153.85	192.31
24000	4.62	23.08	46.15	69.2	92.31	480.00	184.62	230.77
30000	5.77	28.85	57.69	86.5	115.38	600.00	230.77	288.46
40000	7.69	38.46	76.92	115.4	153.85	800.00	307.69	384.62
50000	9.62	48.08	96.15	144.2	192.31	1000.00	384.62	480.77
60000	11.54	57.69	115.38	173.1	230.77	1200.00	461.54	576.92
70000	13.46	67.31	134.62	201.9	269.23	1400.00	538.46	673.08
80000	15.38	76.92	153.85	230.8	307.69	1600.00	615.38	769.23
90000	17.31	86.54	173.08	259.6	346.15	1800.00	692.31	865.38
100000	19.23	96.15	192.31	288.5	384.62	2000.00	769.23	961.54
120000	23.08	115.38	230.77	346.2	461.54	2400.00	923.08	1153.85
150000	28.85	144.23	288.46	432.7	576.92	3000.00	1153.85	1442.31
180000	34.62	173.08	346.15	519.2	692.31	3600.00	1384.62	1730.77
200000	38.46	192.31	384.62	576.9	769.23	4000.00	1538.46	1923.08
300000	57.69	288.46	576.92	865.4	1153.85	6000.00	2307.69	2884.62
400000	76.92	384.62	769.23	1153.8	1538.46	8000.00	3076.92	3846.15
500000	96.15	480.77	961.54	1442.3	1923.08	10000.00	3846.15	4807.69

NOTES:

NOTES:

NOTES:

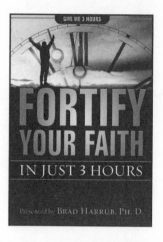

America's Foundation of Faith – Audio CD

Over the past few decades, those who would have you embrace atheistic tenets have been quietly spreading a canard about our government, the Founding Fathers and others who played a key role in the development of America. They have painted them as agnostics, deists, or even atheists. They have worked hard to strip God, the Bible, and Christianity from our public and governmental buildings and even our historical documents. This collection of quotations is a small reminder of the religious heritage of this country. Not only did these individuals embrace God and claim Christianity, they recognized what would happen to a free civil government in which God's commands were ignored. These were the men and women who set this nation on track to becoming the greatest country this world has ever seen. Listen carefully to their words.

Available at focuspress.org

ALSO AVAILABLE FROM FOCUS PRESS

Discover the Truth
– DVD

This exciting video series investigates the claims of evolution and, using scientific evidence, demonstrates how the Genesis record is completely reliable. If you or someone you know has any doubts about the existence of God, this seminar DVD is a must for your personal library.

Disc 1 Includes:
- Was Darwin Wrong?
- Atheism's Attack on America
- Is Genesis a Myth?

Disc 2 Includes:
- The Dinosaur Dilemma
- Scientific Accuracy of the Bible

Available at focuspress.org

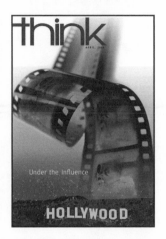